THE
GENERATION
NEW POET SERIES

VOLUME III

Edited by George Abbott White

HARD ROAD NOWHERE

POEMS

HARD ROAI

By R. S. BRONSON

Introduced by *Donald Hall*

NOWHERE

Generation • *Ann Arbor*

ACKNOWLEDGMENTS Thanks are due to the following periodicals in which certain of the poems in this volume first appeared, and who have kindly given permission for their inclusion here: *Arbor, The Paris Review, The Massachusetts Review.*

Library of Congress Catalog card number: 65-23157

Printed in the United States of America.
Published by *GENERATION* under the authority of The Board in Control of Student Publications, The University of Michigan.

Published 4 July 1965
First Edition

This book for the Bronsons

CONTENTS

Introduction

The poetry of R. S. Bronson moves and fascinates me, first and most obviously because it describes a world of which I know nothing: a world of work, of cat six governors and dipper sticks. See "Glossary"; and only the modern Scots poets writing in Lallans have needed a glossary as Bronson does: he writes an American as obscure to me as lowland Scots, and linguistically much more genuine.

But his exoticism, his difference, goes much deeper than subject matter and technical talk; his machines are observed not as alien but as extensions of human feeling. He feels toward diesels the way poets have traditionally felt toward horses or maples. This American comradeship with machinery has never before entered the literary imagination. Take "Barre run":

> *Speed maple leaves against tandem axle*
> *diesel Mack, whorl reddening stack exhaust.*

Poems of skid row, of physical pain like the one about the accident at the missile base, poems of farm living, and poems of family love. This is a world here which is an alternative to the world of other contemporary poets, and to be welcomed for its difference as well as for its literary success. Some of these poems seem naive to me, technically naive and therefore unspeaking. A few of them scrape on my ear like chalk on a blackboard. At other times these notes of a locked self, these dense clotted images move with an inward sureness, and create a man talking whom I have not met in poetry before.

DONALD HALL
20 February 1965

11

Your handwritten love
desk's oldest belonging now
distant unchanged words.

Crabtree

Pumping heart be organ yet. Staminate
spore from gnarl, knot-bark leaf spray whose boy,
hid in topmost crotch, watches him taw,
knelt to oval toed through Greenway dust.
Pumping, heart reform its own. Sons shinny
while petals drop, crouch as apples seed
hillslope toward road, watch themselves shoot taws,
knelt to oval in begotten dust.

Storm

In half this afternoon the hard law parts us
and leaves recalling our preoccupation
after away, you at the station platform
waving, mindformed anguish softly since then.

Home from School

Brother David, mother's named son,
wearing the leather jacket she bought you,
lent until New Year's, kept me warm.
Now you take back weathered horsehide cut
to fit your shoulders, fleece-lined torso
yours, I lose what we both craved for.
David, where? You travel a thousand miles
to spend two days and overnight.
Years I looked for love in a likeness,
still not wed, you wait because of her?

Funeral

Deep purple bell flare, orange style, green calyx,
a morning-glory,
white and blue ones,
wild ones Gramma grew
outside their kitchen window
Grampa won't grow this spring;
a package of seeds costs ten cents,
tin box saving vines up string.
O Gramma, why not in your time?
Why outside unloving features,
hard times, his asthma, scrimp and scrape?
The Shelburne dances weeknights
and last eastbound train back home,
shoe shop whistle six o'clock,
lunchtime young Anna's laughter;
runaway horse and buggy around through Turners,
holding him reined to the road . . .
Photo still comely proud German maiden,
why not tears?
Never will . . .
What never can be.
Beloved, not grandson, Anna Iokaste.

Telling, After the Auction

(Greenfield, Massachusetts)

Fire hiss oil in burner wicks, glow through cast
iron stove lids, burnish kitchen lamp bulb
gloom where Gramp humps over buckwheat bubbled
brown, steam, smoking bacon grease, slips the thin
spatula underneath, flips a slabjack.
"Well, Robert, we got lots of snow left yet
and cold. Tomorrow's spring. Never nothing
like it here before. We'll come out sometime."
Eye blunt tines, stopped to shovel his sidewalk,
listening, "More snow for tonight. My legs
bother me, being locked up all winter."
Gilded pendulum clicks past fret, glass door;
Africa strikes six hours. "Remember first . . .";
year gone in vacant rooms, Gramp's household spent.

Ripen

Farm outweigh its acreage, reckoned bins;
tilling turns to toil-cribbed seasons' rote,
autumn shade risen in sugar buckets,
oxen prints between, runners groove
plowed snow to mud. Oatstubble, scythe,
hulled walnuts, sideboard berry pie,
harsh northeaster sough,
shouting boys roam lofts
lifelong hands have roofed.

Memorial Day   *(Urbana, Illinois)*

Think about years and the plants, a long while since
roaming this graveyard, buried loved-ones gone,
only quiet, wind through hemlock needles,
afternoon car horn, supper hour twilight,
scuffing dry brown elm leaves, reading headstones.
Buttonwood, often leaned on scaling bark,
dream where no world spins a crinkling leaf,
cellulose torn off veins, whistling Brahms',
staring out as mourners place wreaths, fur neck
overcoats hunched, lonesome follower's step
on just-filled grave, heel sunk in gravel, turf —
whoever there, if you above and I
beneath, feel what? Death not stretched in the dead's
position. Not myself; corpse? After years
and the plants, come back to grave, buttonwood trunk;
you see me leaned toward love and place our wreath.

Quarters of Tomorrow

Hear the woodcock, sad wanderer; know his cry
sounding in you after triumphant moments
turn to night silence. His call answers yours lone
where leafed branches burnt in heaving smoke to sparks,
tree hearts and grasses smolder, wither, sap burst
to steam, deafening yet hear the woodcock's cry,
"Wilderness fledgling, you sought, sparrow at eaves
crouched now when owl from waste places' flight over,
feed on own crumblings, solitude, wept tear drops
and grieve, fled back on overwhelming trouble
to oldest ways where ashes scorch your want stark,
where no one knows you, where no space given you."
The woodcock cries from living, "Understand; our
strength deliver out of charred woods, wanderer,
my passion bountiful with your being love."

Long valley folded by hillslopes, ancient cleft
brook bed, pouring under ground glacial boulders
pooling through days grown cattails, forget-me-nots,
washes sod off bank elm roots, beechfall dried leaves
down rapids grooving shoved granite ledges smooth,
become meadow as goldfinches on brambles,
grasshopper chawing blades, rainbow within you
climbing Green Mountains rock bruised leaping up falls
towards higher shallows till more air than water
where death in what is not yours . . . Drop back, slick-trout,
to deep flows, sand bars, worn round gravel rippling,
slowly mouth your own swift passage through your gills
while a painter sits here hours, his mind holds sights,
his hand brushes colors that wind rufflings fix
and sun bakes, oil brook him in your larger force.

19

We were together, one live with worded love
not knowing to reply, who dwelt on your lips,
nonentity among men, though never seen
nor named nor pitied in their passings, dreaming
"I am born at your touch, taken from womb, nursed
at light singing breaths into morning blood's pulse;
your being beats through my veins, muscles weighted
with trusting; creation, spill out happiness,
cup uttering songs . . . " longing, eyelids wink tears
on useless hands, seemingly red-bound book bleeds
rain on chokecherry leaves outside, whisper
fear that courses swollen hollow-chest sorrow,
my makeshift arms gripping own ribs, ankles crossed,
haunches on unpainted boards, rocker empty,
I read definitions: the words for love you.

If we two are together, then we have strength
among millions whom I have found to embrace
by loving You, knowledge to face them from You
though crowding sweaty hands grapple, elbows jab,
sour hot mouths spew spit, men and women jostle,
chortle, their gestures strained beyond themselves mob
that stares at the corpse extended above them,
chest sinews taut, legs bracing heels against wedge,
firm arms outstretched, at stained loincloth abdomen
hard with last pain; Soul, whose want puts hunger down
tenderly while they gouge their quarry, fiercely
bleed dead heart dry but still beneath what these see
fail transform shouting, sufferers each a life
pulled from no height and wound in labdanum sheet,
mine Hallelujah since You have livened me.

20

Greek Easter *(Verona, Pennsylvania)*

Immutable flickering penumbral,
tallow spattering bronze candelabrum,
mourning undraped and portals opened, we
joyously hallow at midnight, censer
whirling sweet murk risen starward. Clearly
the Patriarch tolls, "Christos anesti."

A Leaf, The Rose *(New York City)*

I am leaf, she no more than scarlet rose,
your remembrance enough while Greek music
and the dancers, old men, quick sons crouched, heels
skipping. Her eyes demand, her soft mouth curved
haughtily Aegean, their mother whirls,
eternal Samos, Crete, Thessaly,
Icarian, Stemnitsote, Athenian
palms over shoulders, circling while their wildest
leader wheels her dancing from his handkerchief.
After feasting and retsina, most loved groom,
do you recall this transient xenos ever
or your fervent Syrian girl? Bring me the most
expensive wines; I pay for the eyes you loved once.
Now Helene sips the amber wine,
dark eyes' laughter, strokes your greying curls.

Manhattan Nights

Sunday:
Who mocked black till brought among blues records,
tasting the hog tripes with greens, and cocktails
on New Year's night danced Sylvia, Negress
become love, learning between umber lips.
Drunkenly led from her art, rave apart.

Monday:
If, be a haven. From Twenty-third Street
catch an Uptown train and watch for their eyes
as far as one replies who leaves the car
at Grand Concourse. Follow until she meets
her suede-foot beau outside the turning stiles.
One token saved, buy three chocolate bars
to while away riding down the island.

Tuesday:
Though other guys stood talking,
thinking out loud, "Are we for nothing?",
fear kept me walking city streets.
Then I stopped. Why want worth?

Wednesday:
Precarious brownstone face mortar,
brick wall, quarters a sixth floor front room,
window on Amsterdam. Deny
plaster cracks, brindle moulding,
warped boards by bedding strewn, worn books
unshelved, socks and trousers scattered
on periodicals, shape your own space,
read "Vixit . . . ", pent among million renters
where the Authority condemns these blocks.

Thursday:
Amorous doubt reflecting window shoppers,
glass front to Macey's Christmas toys, your moist lips
glisten tinsel, a last-minute purchase joy.

Friday:
White amidships, green fore, red aft
glide between Weehawken Ferry docks,
a barge crane huffs out steam, gears wind
cable, clam shell dredging muck
at Lincoln Tunnel. Hudson River
sewage, jetsom, liner's winches
hoisting crates and tourist cars. Empty
semis rumble, steel jar on cobbles;
overhead Westside traffic and plane wings
flash red, white, green. Homeward workman's
grimace, spitting out harsh exhaust,
engine grime on grim lips.

Saturday:
Leaned on the concrete railing, we stood talking
while some drifted, were drifting past and by us
again through street and sign light gloaming; brown rats
below scuttled down walks in yew shrub shadows.
Watching them chase, we grinned. I told him surely,
"You never meet that self you want alive,
though some will seem to be the love you thought."
We talked until eleven when he drifted
to choose among them. Only I stood, certain.

Rage at Weeping

A mother
owns the apartment below my room,
whips her son,
runs him out of her parlor into her kitchen,
cringes him behind the stove,
writhes him beneath the sofa,
screams the swing of her black strap, slaps him sharply
last night, this morning and now,
anger, hate shouting loudly.

What did he do
to her,
to her furniture, home, neighbors, friends, mind,
to her owning him?
He can never run farther than her locked doors,
love, thrash strap tyrrany curb-moulding hers.
At least stamp downstairs and smash her door,
stop that social right to rear her own,
beating him along the kitchen floor linoleum.

What could he have done,
what could any of us have done to ruin this system,
yet each in his own reasoning cube cringes;
bulge breasted mother beats hers righteously.

What done?
Each of us has tried to be his own
though none is anymore.

Until in bed he cries chokingly;
she shouts, "Be still or feel the strap again.",
silent child inside her room,
          inside her home,
          inside her own,
but not himself, not his own. Never.

Of Leaving Again

Steeple clock springs wound,
unwound times thousand,
belfrey bells
sound down through this town,
echoes bounding, pastures, hills.
One . . .

                        six . . .

                                        twelve o'clock.

Another hour gone,
bronze clappers rumbling in the well of steeple stones,
timed ticks pounding,
resound to meet around a day a night.
My heart measures each beat
as steadily as blood returns —
                        heart
artery   capillary   vein
heart —
so hands wind round,
so springs wind down,
twelve . . .

                        six . . .

                                        one o'clock,

bell echoes through the town,
rooftops to belfry,
Mondays to Sundays . . .
Always I am bound
outward and away
while bell sounds echo bell sound
until time, blood pulsed,
returns,
heart wound
and wounded times thousand.

Will Identity *(Ann Arbor, Michigan)*

This evening no cars stop. Who ride? Crippled
hound risen feebly limps along the road
homeward, once more hit, broken then under
running tires. Who steer? You pity its try,
swerve clear. Remind; Chinese venerable struck
at Eighth and Twenty-third, Manhattan noon,
bloodily stretched on asphalt, fumbles hands
to put a half pound square of butter back
in the ripped paper bag. Though dying, brain
still order. Who drives? In right of way, whine
and twitching forelegs strain to stay alive.

Epitaph for Brenstafn

Boot throttle, double clutching to seventh
diesel crankshaft revs twenty-one hundred,
tandem drives and semitrailer axles,
tires against the Weaver Mountains grade
northbound for Prescott. Snowstorm six years past,
him driven toward desert, westcoast cities,
counting on a tramper for New Zealand,
bellyfull of chocolate cake and coffee,
windscoured granite above the cafe, shoes
wet in drifts, dawn reddens rimrock timber,
cactus hooks his leg again, blood rubbed
on thumb, venturer who left lectures, bookstacks,
Rackham Hall quartets and willed himself free ways,
eases on airbrakes, truckstop lights ahead.
Rig parked and idling, open that same door.

Es muss sein. Better believe intellect
hardens and muscles chest, thickens forearms,
biceps shouldering khaki shirt seams torn,
ruins what the unsearchable disposed.
"Ultimate penalty be death.", savage
hatred thin youth whose classroom ideas,
student voice citing Piers, Jungian heroes,
ocean-rough sonnets work this trucker's road.
"Hey, gorgeous. Steak." "Hi. Where you headed."
"Prescott. Much farther?" "Thirty-six miles."
"Stopped here once years ago, first trip."
"I just been working three months."
"Blizzard forced me off Sixty-six.
Bright desert and highway straight out west,
figured I was over the mountains then.
Ended in Honolulu, dead broke."
"I'd love to travel." "Come on to Prescott.
Soon's they unload me . . . "

Injectors not pumping, valve cams
stopped, parking brake locked, he logs off-duty.
In the cab sleeper, after seven shots
downed at Elkhorn Bar with joking ranch hands,
callused fingertips at temple, this driven
trucker's metrical heartbeat spoken
breaths onto windshield frost crystals . . .
"You then, hear my voice
in the sound of these words,
my own voice, my own self
in these words here tonight.",
hand outstretched toward ashtray pencil slumps, at last
      sleep.

Barre Run

Speed maple leaves against tandem axle
diesel Mack, whorl reddening stack exhaust.

Day Gone

Two laborers talk
about antifreeze, puddle
ice under one's truck.
Steak and mushroom feed,
phonograph folksong warm doze;
anxious latest lips.
Rose Bar closed at two,
sweat socks wetting the chair back
and empty rubber boots.

Skinner Blues

What'm I gonna do
now I broke up with you?
Going disengage the clutch
and try some other gear.
You my speed no more,
my low-low no more.

Break

Idle hunting diesel six, dozer down
and left cat braked. Sprawl skinner akimbo,
sandwich wrappers to fill, emptied thermos
between oiled boots, dream him twelve mile in town.

Jukebox guitar blow shitkicking. Bar slop
and beer rings smear under forearms. Blunt, grease
blackened nails scratch thick wrist hair. Tip draft.
Cut for two bills. Splayed callus finger watchfob.
"Buddy and me hauled sawlogs through them parts.
Ugliest bitch ever. Took her out 'hind
the cafe. Snow come on, wind ahowling,
planked that hellcat up again' her backhouse.
Me and him drove. Trinities, Glenn Canyon.
Up to Butte till he got too much of grit
in his teeth. Need to chew ponderosa;
go fat on this dam job." *Miss you, ole boy.*

Woken, engine hour mean r.p.m.'s. Stretch
hard shoulder tendons, lever throttle wide.

The Hard Go

Shovel man runs grade, station four plus nought-nought
cut nineteen feet. Erie Fifty-one bucket
loads shot rock to Euc backdumps hot ten hour day.
Jimmie two-cycle whines acceleration.
House swinging, Doug bumps the Cat six governor,
dumps and swings back. Teeth crowding slate shard,
    two yard more.
Dipper sticks clear the cab; driver props skived boots
on his westcoast mirror. Trip; Doug waves him out.
The oiler, "Joker wants to set here all day."
"Yeh, he's lazy.", foot braking whipline, "Teamster
on the Thruway called their business agent in,
New York gangster, bitched about me loading fast.
Outfit had four drivers. Told him I'd work six,
good digging. He chewed that guy's butt. 'What you bring
me way out here for! The operator's right.'
Next day we got two men. Driving to my room
that night, engine seized up. Barstard poured sugar
in my crankcase. I stayed. They sweat in and out
the cut, no waiting fifteen minutes to load.
There's no brotherhood, Oiler. Even your friend
will cry to the Hall, you got the job he wants."
"They done o.k. by me, Doug.", wipes grease off zirks.
"Before I joined this local, twenty years back,
run dozer in Acadia, paid eighty cents.
All put up at the same boardinghouse. Raised hell
nights with the owner and her maid. Cadillac,
Rockefeller inside, was on the job once.
Could own one now myself. No good to show off.
Whitie, master mac down to Long Island, run
off two scraper men. Flashed their checks in a bar
where lawyers, doctors drink. Spend years at college,
make the wage some dumb skinner does." Compressor

horn blows noon. Boom lowered, stretching, fingers comb
grey hair; Doug saunters to his new Pontiac.
Oiler on the saddle block yells to three Euc
drivers squatted in a rig's shade, "Deal me in,
Scotty. Old lady give me five bucks for gas."

Accident, Atlas ICBM Base

" . . . what has passed for nature has not passed for mind."
A. N. Whitehead, *THE CONCEPT OF NATURE*

Fall morning groundfog shrouds Rocheberg missile site
while graveyard labor steward, the drill doctor,
tagman lift him, corpse bones broken, smashed skin
wound in bloody denim coveralls, sock torn.

Shot stone, riser hole, ring beams foot stilled workmen,
traxcavator engine idling, bucketload
raised. Three ton scale pan up slowly, wire rope hoists
through mist; silo walls them one hundred sixty feet.
Overhead point sheave bearings spin in grease,
boom, Ten-ten house swing, diesel exhaust bellows.
Operator, watch soft handling beside gouged
welded plate steel, four cross compacted rock fill
toward their hoghouse. "Oiler. Shut the rig down."
"Not your fault, Ray. Tagman says that boy jumped off
a ring beam just as your pan set on the shot.
Didn't know he was underneath till John seen
his hardhat and boot.", head walker stands outside
on cat pads, pocketed left hand jingling coins.

"Tell the Super I took a walk.", whipline brake
locked, Ray comes off the hundred ton crane front, leans
against Euc backdump, breathing eased, hearing,
"Sonofabitch foreman fired me five o'clock.
Told us to set steel other side that link fence
barrier where they was loading muck. 'Either
work or get run off.' I weren't going under
no damn bucket. The poor kid done like he said.
Two month Leon's pushed us to beat Stanton site.
Even so, they'll blame the guy for being there."

"You o.k.?", khaki workclothes, cigar smoke drift,
field superintendent's palm cups Ray's shoulder.
"Tough break, son. Go ahead home; phone me tonight."

Take off among dayshift men coming on past
toolshed, hoghouse, Engineers' office trailer
to the grey Buick convertible bought last spring,
"Poor damn bastard, you.", key turned in ignition.
Drill doctor to master mac, Ray driving out
the gate, "Ten bucks he don't climb back on that rig."

Bootsole against throttle reving Cat crankshaft next
graveyard shift, sweaty fists grip drum and swing levers,
drillers in the birdcage lowered to bottom out.
Cowboying burnt bands unafraid night ago, shout,
"Oiler, tell the tagman I can't see his hand."
Nonspin line unspools up white boom frame, down
        through groundfog.

Northwest, Year After Dozer School

Fir timber Snake's somber slopes. Soberly,
Oley and John, remember Kleinschmidt Grade,
cat dozed snowfault north from Oxbow damsite,
road green rusted Olds through turns, rockfall wash,
while our boasts; December skinners number
jobs. Brushrake busts elm roots, Vermont burnish
towards Camels Hump powder frost cap. Stumper
belong to Myrtle Point, Coquille lumber
where Carol's amber eyes repeat her gift
last Christmas night, lips still whispering, "Steve."

Watch and Vibrocompactor *(Montpelier job)*

Eight o'clock unwinds shock resistent ticks,
Lima fob adangle from denim watch
pocket, daylong sound. Crudely, hate seep out
work learnt hurt to lever machine bound pads,
gear teeth, clutches, brain. Goshawk rend fieldmouse
flesh on pole crossarm. Below, by spring clicks,
tamp parkinglot gravel towards four-thirty.

Deed *(Littleton, New Hampshire)*

Veined rigid bulge, thick inner forearm strength
whose musclings loaded pan, shifted diesel
fire to tire lengths down half mile grade, stretch hand
for none that rods scraper on this damn fill.
Work quit, will them the haul roads.

Operation

Worn darned shirt hung up, bare shoulder,
surgeon's needle threading cut skin to again.

Loss Recalled

Told him, "Be hunter or run hunted. Fear smell
makes them attack.", by executive, swimmer.
Sun through their beer glasses glints yellow shafts
on callused dread and vital scars, the wrecked boy.

Destroyer *(Boston, Massachusetts)*

Hook hobbed bootheel over Jake Wirth's brass rail,
elbow propped to walnut bar. Poured liquor,
around the four bit clinking till's cashier
loud talk, rawkus, hoarse; down the bottle raw shot
while New Year's noon. Wheels tells his latest cruise.

"Had calm weather going down to Gitmo.
Jesus, was it hot! Took some time to whip
our crew in shape." "This one on the house.", rag
wiped through bar spill. "During them battle problems,
in helmets, life jackets, shirt sleeves rolled down
and buttoned, twelve men cram the pilot house.
Then I move to the windward side, throw a leg
over the bulwark, sametime hot and cool.
Plotting from the bridge an hour, I'd spotted
old beacons, lights and mountain tops again.
We practiced shore bombardment steaming out
to rendezvous. Taking bearings I felt
funny, stumbled back. Phones slipped off my head.
Draped an arm through the porthole; couldn't think.
Someone yelled, 'Kip's going.' Captain jumped up
and grabbed me from behind. Couple more here, Tom."

Ringing two sales, fat blonde pets permanent waves.
"Docked at Port au Prince for Change of Command,
the skipper broke it off in the Commodore
who sat down there in front. Highest squadron
marks was Eight-O-Two's. He gave another Can
the 'E'. Our Old Man was on their shitlist.
Two waiters handle kraut and knockwurst, mirrored.
"One more calendar page, I'm through with this hitch.
Sure miss the ole boy. He worked at skinning cats.
Things we done, places we seen broke or flush;

we planned to head for Canada, later
Alaska. I got more than most First Class,
charthouse to myself, sleep there, work alone,
no duties but navigation. So damn sick
of the sea! Match you for double shots, bud.",
bourbon trickle over his skinned knuckle grip.
"Lonesome life to hell and gone in the sticks.
Till lately he never drunk much. Asked him once,
possible to flip that rig. When I think back,
Frisco, Dago, we drove our cycles rain
or dust storms. Bud had plans before we happened
to meet; no doubt. He stopped his travels to wait.
It was Australia Buddy had in mind.
November, his last letter shook me up.
Got a passport after he wrecked his scraper.
Jesus, I sure felt bad to get such news.
Taxi delivered me downtown San Juan.
Roamed some crib bars. Ran on this one cafe,
good looking native owner talked in French,
fast old Haitian accent. Caught what she meant
most of the time drinking her rum." Anxiously,
boy cadge,   "Shine 'em, swabbie?" Shoe on his box,
"Don't remember leaving the Carribe Hotel.
Guess I passed out cold in their low bar lounge.
Upped anchor Thursday, 'Desig U.S.A.'
flying off the outboard yardarm.", pulls dollars
from blues' jumper; smoothed between blackened palms.
"No banner flew for the most decent buddy
ever. You savvy? Hope he's done all right.
Much water over the dam. A loner again.
Going through with building a cabin though.
But my best hopes went with Bud. If someday

he's down and out can come chop and split wood
on my farm. Just hope he ain't gone too damn long.
Jesus, I'd fed with this life. So sick!
Too fouled up for talk, bud. So long."

Whitehat weave out Stuart Street doorway. Shift
hobbed boot, fingers signal barkeep for dark,
quietly drunk watching beer flow. Buddy,
notice olden words carved above the glass,
Suum Cuique, mirroring this passage.

Trace *(Richmond, Vermont)*

Accoutered log-idea span one more;
engineers bridge Winooski River. Still
at noon gulls hunch on gravel spits — iron
workers, carpenters eat in girder shade
and talk; words add little to that first thought
though here the print shows prestressed concrete decks—
then course shifting riffles while weather flakes,
loads wear construction. Wage and labor spent,
jaw gaped corpse, who lodged them trues to straightedge
stock again with the next sons' journey grips.

Freshen *(Greendale, Vermont)*

Molecules flame off hearthstone granite, cool
in woodash. Slower combustion leans to warm
cupped palms at the bright energic course, coals
aglow with dawn-tinged cumuli, earthen grown
through elm seeds, felled and hewn. Their primal source
re-formed to split boles burnt, aged thoughts fired, force
timelessly changed withstands itself: swelling
fungus spores harm; matured, quintillion new cells
disease, dooryard trees' own end. Shadow boughs
thresh in his handbricked flue where wintry gusts sough.

"They Will Survive"

Talus, benches, alluvial fan — rain
water runoff carrying quartz back down
toward tidal mud; once before this granule,
roiled in storms, settled out near trilobites,
now where three boys shovel their castle moat.
Knowing what will happen again, Kotcho,
gently kiss your sons while all of you are.
George bends, ear to sea swells; Nick strokes shallows
on earth's archaic abyss; Steve's hands splash —
moment over and begun forever.

Harsh Unbinding   *(District of Columbia)*

Has none's world tract to purpose and content
where killing be extinct, then not the men
today yet Man whose unfleshed minds know his
cosmos, historic wants forgotten since
this plaza fountain bathed rude poorboys splashing,
coloreds' with whites' shouts; t-shirt taut at blades,
muscular forearms crossed on bent knees, brow
bedded to thick worker wrists, statuesque
conqueror profile stills, broken bum down
off granite turned bronzen slough though Washington,
Pulaski stride, water babies will try
and hunker murdered past their thirties so
till ages wizen lusts whose kind evolve
learned charities to love, his inherent.

Value (*Great Smokies*)

. . . hour, has become embodied in the cotton,*
another in this hike up Blanket Mountain;
daylong marketed, bought up, banked, consumed
or sweat on paths worn up toward dreamed-of views.

*Karl Marx: *DAS KAPITAL*

Forgotten Succession *(Paradise Key, Florida)*

Not along this trail, but through another
anhingas swim searching out bream and pout.
Plank walks bound the hammock whose tangled old way
struggle in water, mankind's 'Taylor Slough';
splash, then broken wingbeats, fright squawked . . .
    Listening,
start above an uncoiled cottonmouth,
uneasily saunter back to the parkinglot.

Ranges *(Cape Sable, Florida)*

Barred owl among these crows hooks on bleached
    mangrove
tatter where hurricane blasted ocean flood
swamped the jungle, strokes against her wings' wind
eying bare sweeps, then stoops, glides west and perches
while their caws call, bating till carrion drops
past aerial roots. Stronger than cyclonic
cloudbursts whorled calmward, breaths' laws uniform
    men
to watch those threatened, owl among dogged crows,
by our persistent species' growth, exploit
that daily devours guarding its own new worlds,
glade for like but preternatural coursing.

Creators (Altar Society Benefit, Big Pine Key, Florida)

Through eons polyps form reefs, mangrove roots
bar the neap tides sifting sediments out,
palmetto, slash pine leaf, moulder; campground
by Spanish Harbor, bingo games, fried fish
mix northern tourists, natives, nuns and priest.
Ray spreads tent flaps, holds the bracelet-necklace
prize toward his friend who sits with Gibbon's Rome.
"Why'd you eat with them; you're not Catholic now."
"Nope." "Nor Protestant." "Not that either." "What you
believe in, helping their cause like that?" "Myself.
The sun there, this can of beer, label . . . " Sun and
beer gone, whatever earth spins as, Ray spends his.

A Thing

We ordered ourselves to fire that burnt before,
blazed because of, and flames despite our purpose,
tended, worshiped, intensified to work,
to bloom on foes: of us, some fought by others.
Live by sun-fusion, taught by its examples,
urges in our historic kind's short while
threatened to ruin, "Aught revolve through starlight
when human thought consumes the earth no longer?"
Blast extinguish civilization's force,
national bounds then desert ground and sky
where, rising with the solstice moon, spring tide
Atlantic flows on changing shorelines, slowly
recedes, Pacific seas bulge forward, both
erode our harbor landmarks, none who regrets?

45

Being Only Now

At prey through darting shoals of minnows, snapper
spun out on beached burnt rockweed, silver wriggling
thrown back in channel wash to continue live,
never fathom what hand is that lifts and flings
nor I what cosmos beyond our present ken.
In caused ways, pursuit to wave warped oolite,
neither clench fist nor shout against easterlies
but seer once more wait out desperation,
hours for time-sense, whose mind endure searchingly
toward that next depth and height my reason attempts.
So law-bound grow, epochal change through countless
successive selves, limited form suggesting
futures not own while against my nearing end
I try inside still rudimentary man.

Purpose Beyond Now

Along the river brontosaurus track
on red mud; when THEIR age is, Hamlet found,
Sermon on the Mount, or other traces
petrified from passed man's succeeding mind,
strain of being through Lao-Tzu and more
whose will create for no earth life but ours.

Intrusives *(Casa Grande de los Chisos, Texas)*

Molten stone flow cooled and hardened, gale updrafts
scouring sand on shrink cracks an eon, lichens
carbonating ledge to slope rockfall, flash flood
washed cobbles gouging draw, arroyo, canyon
till buttress column weathers out through billion
orbit planes in galactic whorl while atoms
become you, mortal only knower here not
learning end of change, specific intellects
reason kit fox, sotol, rhyolite order
out of earth's from which you have grown, eroded
butte peak to Rio Bravo silt, gulf strata,
then yours the archaic brain whose own event
disperse with variform course, elements once
combined in consciously searching heritance.

Structural *(Yavapai Point, Grand Canyon)*

Haunt Coconino scarprock where iron rails
lip vibrant gravity. Earthwind blows long, clouds
the sunset event reddening sandstone, jays
on pinyon. Motion of subatomic force,
particular trembles self beneath this scalp,
wears granite eons under Tonto Platform.

Quaternary Descent

(South Kaibab Trail, Grand Canyon)

Nimbo-stratus snowsweep onto Supai butte
cedars, redwall stain beneath, where one man walks
down from earliest reefs, trilobitic shale
raven perch passed, toward Inner Gorge
where Pacific slope outflow slots this domed plateau,
his silent pause at inert billion year old
crystalline silt, magma fractures through buckling
schistose range worn to submarine cores, sage here
sonoran mate from theirs in white roar, rapid
gravel and sand that grinds the course of spring thaw
pouroff bedding fossil events on last laid
floodplains, he encounters the rockbound era
when matter, regardless its search in his evolved
sense how, began to be live; sudden fist clench stone.

Pervious *(near Bullion Mountains, California)*

Animate scared, Mohave wastes in him,
desert sheers, futilely stood on a blown
torn erosion, incline washed out from scarps,
worn son among lava strata arroyos,
tilted limestone bluffs, tastes his salt tears. Needles
under alto-cumuli layering north,
mesa, alluvial flats darken. Air
scouring draw walls slithers sand in fault cracks;
grains swept crosswise blind him. Only this while,
learn, nothing else aware in stinging earth here.

48

Increase   *(Crystal Cave, Sierra Nevada)*

Yellow grinders blunted down in gums till
gaunt buck mule deer struggles under coyotes
slashing haunch strings, fang torn muscles bolted,
hooves thresh, crush green browse on bloodied oakleaf
mold, not willingly inert again as
flesh digests gulped vigor. Archean force
through varying form, hikers stone them off,
phone the ranger station. Rifle slugs rip
softened panting, air lung-sucked toward vitals
blown, immortal change where Marble Fork pours.

Fitting Determinants

Propped against brick building corner become
my impossible and crosswalk white lines, electric
red, then amber, green as horns honk, engines
oxidize hydrocarbons to heat, sounds, odors,
I can sense nothing outside this valence exchange
but what is harsher guess for our pre-ylem
origin how until now in unknowing increases
live through space, short slow growth to progeny whose
loving may theorize light beyond their God,
others than pedestrians heeding boards,
cosmic rays trajecting solar fusion
while Venus scintillates through mare's-tails above roofs
though where they and I walk, macro-molecular
protein events, no mind understands nor why yet.

At The Corner Light (San Francisco)

Fillmore alleyway window frame fat woman,
drunken, at kitchen greasy oil cloth table
half gallon carton of milk and a fifth. Dark,
wrinkled, thick knuckles hold her fast; four pink nails
grip to empty chipped jelly glass. Through all night
till the bells toll Sunday reason told go free,
feel breasts young, buttocks hard in new straw and him
come back by Fleishhacker Zoo under date palms.
Got none but herself, stare from shoe on dust rolls
down to blue chiffon, child who brings the Bible
for school sole stir, lovely above harbor fog.

Worth *(San Francisco)*

Bum another drink on Embarcadero
where scrufty ladies shuffle, winos belch bile
vomit, smash emptied pints against brick storefronts.
Bight of the line whip across John's chest; nipple,
bowel skin split, gut bulge through ripped cowboy shirt,
black belt, chrome Cat buckle, denim fly bloody.
"I was swamper for the dozer yarding stumps.
Cable busted at the clevis hitch, come back
on me fore there was time to blink. Give a guy
one more swig off that bottle, Bud. They sewed up
my belly but the old back don't work right yet.
Thanks, friend, this stuff keeps the ache down. Goddamn
     rain !
Can't bend over nor lift nothing too heavy.
Year ago I was one strong sonofabitch.
Well, Bud, I got to find a empty car, sack out."
Bared head, dampened hair and overcoat, preacher
gently touch his sleeve, "You need a place tonight."
"On your way, bible-banger. We don't count." "Son,
despite those words, you count to men of good . . ." "Scram.
All you bastards want to chalk up'nother bum."

Oath

Drive that hellbent semi, good buddy, Frisco
to Phoenix run once more though corpse lay buried
under family's bouquets, outfit's floral
wreath and dirt six feet, meet in time for double
shots before we hit the rack. God damn me lone.
Who give road, rush load, blowout and driver dead?
What rotgut sousing'll stop this bitter mouth?
McCarthy's place, mouse-face empty stool, ashtray,
glass, flat beer. Rawkus whore, laugh; wino, slobber.
Build you one sure everlasting monument
inside my head, old boy, where none can bother,
me and you will smoke cigars and talk times past;
till they yard us off this body's yours to live.
Sober up, quit the skid, find a redwood shack
near Klamath, no more waiting. Bud, drive that rig.

Bequest to the Wino   *(Seattle's skid road)*

Mother, if I could be your child again,
lay my head upon your lap in dreaming;
soft warm fingers stroke my hair so slowly . . .
No! Without friend or wife, this hardened hatred
smiles no answer to interest a waitress,
no words for the sympathetic bartender.
Waterfront hotel room's sweet tokay reek,
bedside bottles, mattress smolder around
the cigarette between my fingers glows
again. Do I holler till the nightclerk pounds
to wake me if he's not drunked up or hold tight,
choked as flames burn hotter, dresser and wall fired,
raw smoke deleriums? O Mother, this
was not mine when I had no fear of you
and lay still, dreaming on your gentle lap.

Plaint *(Mount Olympus, Washington)*

Earth endures her own storms, destroys again
and recreates a ravaged visage whole.
Noblest woman, O world, I who loved you
while dying blood spurt through my nostrils, hand
flung out to touch your calmness, felt harsh whisper
in broken eardrums, sharper, lips at jawbone
splinters, then leaf fall cover and mold about
the calcic part resisting blowfly maggots,
my living gone. Become wherever in yours,
vast quantum chemic, I could say how cruel
teeth behind thick kisses clamp, chew hotly,
how they ground my throat that was yours as well.
Mother, build me into other suitors;
so, I will still show mine as fiercely true.

"Westward on the
high-hilled plains . . ." *

Where Easthampton bounded, my growth began,
changing blood spurts strong through newer ways now
who strip and dive from Manhan claybank elm crotch,
swim the river run to Gulf Stream rain clouds
re-forming flows past their sons' slippery race
up paths to brink and leaps I turned away from,
no boy mine that shouts from long descending
and rise, no brother's hand to splash him then
as being me live still atoms tread afloat
when I lie, separate particles inert
again until ones joined with animate force
transform while soul, though deathlike infinite change
an essence split and same whose township grave
worn toward seas may never be place to found,
revive beyond those more human than my means.

*A. E. Houseman: *A SHROPSHIRE LAD*

In-selves

Think proud robins nest the chokecherry fork
for fledgelings? Pride your own gestalts for that,
four hatched out of blue eggshell among shrill
cluckings, earthworms, budded blades become crow's,
lilac scent cold evening traffic rushes
past streetlamp gleamflow; neither to nor from,
pointillistic video-imagery crowds
pair flickering sofa gloom and voidlit stares,
wavery curtains blow off distant railroad
upgrade boxcar lugged diesel oil burnt regret,
day you painted the pantry cupboards, walls,
ceiling, window, door, and mouldings — past pots,
dining set, shade roller, vase, breadmixer . . .
After washing and drying dishware then take
iced tea, inhaling your own enamel air.

Preparers for Decoration Day

We four have been together quite a while;
now you folks set to buy a graveyard lot,
Dave and I left, tending to potted plants,
to keep on, whose when ours are gone? Way back.
birthday picnic and Christmas suppertime
still there then besides the remembering
what we went through, family gathered, countless
what before is
what afterwards
not just through abuilding decayed
but always light —
screened porch at home, night talk an hour till bed,
bodily gestures where we will leave them old;
we four have been together quite a while.

George and Anna Parker

May orchard apple and leaf falls, haysweet lovers
never returning, broken spray blossoming pink
in milk bottle tapwater same heartbeat older —
his tired worn body asleep in the easychair
sunbeams, train westbound boyhood salt-and-pepper suit
cap blown to prairie dog town... Happy birthday, Gramp.
Daughter, her husband and son, hands' veined brown
    blotches again.
Ocean air across Berkshire Hills an oakleaf dry rustling,
warm bee drone bough wind shower stonewall moss petals,
minute crawler vanished between grey slate flag and shoe
    tread —
after the burial past thirteen years old grave
Green River Cemetery lot dried sod, granite headstone,
corpse, O Grandmother, us all light, only brightness . . .
Downhill turned towards town at last your burial
    afterbirth.

Dreams his Grand Canyon

Grandeur Point:

Rimrock sun, cricket . . .
shoe grate on cinder walk stopped,
earthshadow chirping.

North Rim:

Cloudfog dimmed ponderosa bole needles
then brick zodiacal light, Point Sublime
revolved sky watcher on stone together
waterstars' way in myriad nightlong dewdrops,
canyon silence vast moonlit river eons
deep and the Milky Way . . .
                                    Sunrays, slit
between storm and mesa butte, wake him to dawn.

Inner Gorge:

Ubiquitous fly,
front legs wiping its eyes clear,
river boulderfield.

Phantom Ranch:

Troglodyte, wren shrill
canyon songnotes descending
dusk's satellite glint.

Over Wall Creek:

Cottonwood shade and chuckawalla and hiker,
Tonto haze still, spiral on-whirling sand
epoch eroded Cheops Pyramid
blown dust-devil, August day grown dusk,
ominous cumulo-nimbus obscures mute shafts,
upswollen thundercloud red sundown trailing
downpours, deserted dry wash water rush
pound near, muddy torrent rolling boulders.
Yellow pine crown flail, discharging bolt clap,
rainflecked night-bloom, east anvil thunderheads'
sheet lightning glow flares toward Wupatki then Page.

Sun's Four Shields:

Juniper pool:
afterimage morning star
and cottonwood leaf.
Wash stain purplish red
streaks down buff Coconino
sandstone cliffs elate.
Bonded particles'
order knowing agave
stalks sprout yellow, him.
Under Plateau Point
lookoff dry corn storage bins
and stonework ruined.
Where Bright Angel fault
weathered-out canyon crossing
now same force learn so.
Schist two billion years,
sego lily overnight

and the river red.
Mesquite scent moment
dark canyon trail turn sudden
early morning light.
Metamorphosed Brahma
columnar desert varnished schist,
oldest new for him.
Sun warmed Clear Creek bank
one another's twisted down
cottonwood budding.
What back of these
soil and rain and prickly pear
blossom odors?
Sweat up packmules hitched
to catclaws chewing stripped off
bark in flower shade.
Upswung axe sunbursts
under tufted cottonwood
seeds drifting away.
Log corral at dusk,
six head bunched around hay bales,
their skinner outside.
Dry trail: wrangler's
tincan under redrock catch
for limewater ooze.
Doodlebug craters
in trail sand: far skyline
Humphreys and Sunset.
The Colonnade's reds
and yellows shedding talus,
quaking aspen buds.
Autumn campground by
mountain root creekbend empty,

first quarter moon dear.
Stormtail gusts golden
aspen scatter on snow scuff,
nimbus dayglow dim.
Late sun's last warmth drift
snow pink lengthening shadows
its moonlight shortens.
Below icy rails
scarp and gale-soaring raven's
croaking exultant.
Sandstone monument
sunshadow, gnarled juniper
moonshadow, snow squall.
Canyon inert,
only the few mules and men's
way worn north and south.
Roaring Springs cascade
ice and mist and water same
round boulders in thaw.
Winter survey work,
simply one morning hedgehog's
crimson blossom.
Ages sun and moon
shadow around and around
Buddha Temple change.

The Box:

Canyon shaded March grey cottonwoods,
sunlit treetops' bud-green tinge, water spattering
and creek pour over boulder roar Bright Angel
riffles in sandbars, spirogyra strands, willow shoots
and young laborers bellied there drinking,

smooth flat pebble skipped wet rippling glitter,
then wave lap on gravel. Archean bedrock walls.

South Rim Village:

Grand Canyon night silence Labor Day weekend
young drunked up mule skinner whooping at stars.

Tonto Trail:

Ranger's scope sighted
wild burro herd thirst slaking
Pipe Creek rifle shots.

The Colorado:

Nothing a trailcrew foreman
standing at the river dreams
his Grand Canyon; silted swift
current through this same pool too.

Southwest of Four Corners

Teec-nos-pos
nightspeed headlighted old road
walker asphalt wide squaw eyes toward
Betatakin
afternoon whispering groups
evening long shadow spanish
bayonet cream silken lily
spike clump ghost-dust yucca moth gone
Ha-ho-no-geh
canyon tan cocoa grey white
rockbands Navajo weaving hot
Oriabi
rooftop 'dobe eagleperch
turtleshell drier kiva
cacique sunwatch Thriftway Mart
Flagstaff
O that strawberry roan guitar
rye whiskey roamer Bar Sixty-six
Phantom Ranch
dancers to Tennessee Waltz Janet's
scotch on the rocks two billion year once
Bill Williams
northeast slope whiteface juniper range
where deer and antelope . . .
"H'up, little sorrel. Same same's
scrubs got a corral to home."

Water Running Off Mountains

(*June 5 — July 19*)

Across the continental divide, down Canada's western slope, along Olympic Penninsula, then east over the Cascades and Bitterroots back into British Columbia, Alberta, south through Montana, Wyoming, every place people's rivers and mountains now. Sacajawea, Jim Bridger, "Kootnee" Brown walked this country, wilderness once, later Americans' rails, logging outfits, ranches, orchards, their bars, cafes, rodeos, campfires and ours too. When you've been there nothing more, the same one.

Kickinghorse
> Wind river over
> limestone ranges, glacial basins,
> alpine firs' listener.

Beaver
> Meadow evening:
> back and forth cloud's hurrying
> mosquitoes sunlit.

Illicillewait
> Off glacier ice wall
> snowslide roar down moraine side
> momentary ah!

South Thompson
> Kamloops tavern:
> muscled up laborer talk
> soft, cool lager foam.

Fraser
> Railroad bank cave ins
> Pacific winter storm melt
> late night wakenings.

Nooksack
  Before sunup quarter
  section fieldcorn milky groundfog
  first summer moon pondful.

Soleduc
  Morning dim drizzle
  at Salmon Falls—
  continually different
  runoffs, spillway downpour
  only cascade.

Dosewallips
  Hemlock and doug fir
  needles, mossy twigs, cloudmist
  forest floor litter.

Chehalis
  Radiator grid
  swept out tonight, hovering
  white butterflies' day.

Cowlitz
  Gallon Olympic
  springwater flat and too warm
  dumped, Chinook Creek flume.

Tieton
  Canyon night wind and
  burnt pine coals charring rumpsteak,
  fire-hungry dreamer.

Yakima
  Rainier, Adams, Hood
  icefields above the bare Cascades,
  lava bench apples.

Pataha
  Fence corner stud's
  head up gaze, rancher son
  hefting cured bales.

Clearwater
  Broken glass and barstool,
  wives hollering, what starts these guys'
  Cenozoic fistfight?

Lochsa
  Wilderness ridge drifts
  whitewater flood through campfire
  light, snow-wet boots' steam.

Bitterroot
  So many millpond logged
  pines, so many drivers' elbows
  out open car windows.

Flathead
  Ancient sea inland
  grey limestone cirque tarn and spruce
  glacial blue-green.

Columbia
  Sacajawea,
  cupfuls drunk at the Snake back
  along Canal Flats.

Kootenay
  In McLeod Meadow
  marmot's chewed path grass stem squeel,
  smooth quartzite pebble's
  blue butterfly up against
  a washed out denim pantleg.

Oldman
  Redwinged tip's ruffling
  underwater bent cattail
  warble plains daybreak.

Blakiston
  Overthrust bedrock
  upsidedown mountain, "Kootnee"
  Brown's grave Blackfoot ground.

St. Mary
  Piegen halfbreed girl,
  Harwood Bar, drifter picking
  guitar strings, busted.

Sun
  The cottonwood bottoms,
  buffalo bellowing below
  young Lewis, follower.

Missouri
  Cafe window screen,
  wasp inside and fly outside
  trying to get through.

Musselshell
  Plains east-west roadside
  daisy stalk forks goldheaded
  toward dawns and sundowns.

Yellowstone
  Pillar fireball blaze
  green-black cottonwood shadow
  next sweat squinted sight.

Lodge Grass
  Montana summer long
  night journey; wheatfields, hay and beeves
  sweetening thought's nostrils.

Tongue
  Big Horn thunderhead
  raintail east red wet grassland's
  quiet migrant hunched.

Crazy Woman
  Two sag-strand barbwire
  fence barely more than nothing
  but what they stand for.

North Platte
  Prairie dry wash
  country Bridger crossing,
  way away late.

Chugwater
  Lively once tire mashed
  bloody fur's pink jackrabbit
  ear highway heatwaves.

Crow
  Crowded stands shout their
  rodeo cowboy's
  rowels in hard joint
  jarred bronc busting him,
  late afternoon pale moon nightfall sky.

Great Mystery Song

Kachinas (Hopi)

Under thunder southeast dawnlight
white butterfly wings, yellow bean blossoms,
blue cloudflower wetted earth watershine,
shower maidens among cornstalk maidens,
"We please everyone, we please ourselves."
Yellow bean blossom
white butterfly
blue shower
clusters' shining wet young dawnlight men.

Calling Buffalo (Osage)

The grandfather rises —
bull, cow, calf, a scattering,
seven herds from seven directions
arise and stand grazing —
   Curved Sharp Horns
   Humped Withers
   Mighty Flanks
   Tail Bent Back
   Shakes His Mane
   Paws Up Sod
   Earth Rumbler
bounds, hooking side to side, straight on,
hoofprints in plains daybreak everywhere . . .
   "Not now! not now!"
Woman footprints in hilled earth
sprout cornstalk leafsway, green ear
silk plumes, her rising smoke day.

Hogan (Navajo)

Rain Peak, corn pollen white afterglow
upper night over the woman lying down,
mountain-that-calls-men-grandson
mix lightning cloud hail and, snow on springs
our world water, our rainbow's hogan.

Walk Across (Delaware)

Turtlemen's hollow lodges,
            roofbark iced in
                        blizzards;
buffalo, deer and spruce hills east,
Beaver, Bald Eagle, White Wolf fathers'
nightwalk to the Snake Island,
strongest hunters along rich fish shores
over stonehard slippery Tidal Muscle Bearer;
headmen with wives, with daughters and dogs
from the west with hesitation,
daydreaming hollow Turtle lodges,
float their birch canoes upstream through blue spruce
      sunbursts.

Wounded Knee (Dakota)

Father says so, grow on earth song everywhere
sacred pipe smoke many-in-one nation. Shirt
to make live, the dead and buffalo coming,
warriors' dark arrow hunt —
bloody mouths bellow,
staggering legs kick up dust,
    Turn the head, my son.
bright knives cut tongues and hearts out,

71

Hold the shank, my son.
palms rub firesticks, chips smoulder,
    Pull the tail, my son.
 then yellow glow flames . . .
Hey, hey! feasting now,
            eating pemmican.
Come back home, mother, little
brother walks around crying.
Blood friend, what hard hands put on you
                        put on me;
black, bay, buckskin, blue, spotted
all one horse — Dog Soldiers, ghost dancers
pit's red score posts, where stands-beside killed.

Four Point Track (Zuni)

Arroyo chaparral
sun and mule deer crossroads,
hunter's white corn prayer meal,
cigarette smoke blinded
buck — guts on a rock, strong
blood drunk, heart and liver
cooked at camp, piece ground eats —
brought to the cleaned adobe,
blanket over deerhide,
beads around his thick neck,
woman's offering sweetgrass,
buckskin moccasin boots,
an eartip to dead-ones,
venison among the pueblo.
They have taken him into their hearts;
"Hui, hui! Na'le becomes a kachina."

Malpais Sunup (Yaki)

Nighthawk,
mesquite thicket
rotten stick whistling borers' rasp,
three grey dove heads bob.
Just melon root vineleaves,
just stickbug up tendrils stands in a blossom,
canyon ground squirrel chatter loud,
fawn's antler velvet strips,
just cholla juice drip.
Creekhut muskrat hairs on end,
hook-red barrel cactus pears,
just where dry grass shaken
mountainside winds sift dust.
Just a light blue cloud
going up sky
grey with water now
going to break,
thunder mist rains down.

Big Fire's Life (Umpqua)

Pelicans and gulls flown out to sea then
Siuslaw north fork water logs on fire
upriver timber burn along the sky
smoke overcast, whole hot coast range snag flames,
jerked meat and salmon basket rafts offshore,
children in wet canoes ten days red night,
hungry horses, white tail, many elk's burnt
hooves along sand beaches, wading, grizzly
hair scorched off, couger too, island the wolves',
Coyote brought all sorts together. Here it ends.

A Good Way (Kwakiutl)

Ocean
charcoal driftwood,
steelhead skilled at making flesh,
landward round-face tribes'
hemlock boughs in creek pools
salmon run,
smoke dried spawn,
fat round faces
steelhead squirt out making flesh . . .

Glossary:

Acadia—National Park
Africa—pendulum clock
Betatakin—prehistoric ruins
birdcage—elevator hooked to crane line that hoists men
  in and out of the quarry
bottom out—drilled and blasted to construction grade
Bright Angel—creek and canyon
Buddha Temple—butte
bump—push to limit
burnt bands—brake and clutch bands on hoist drums
  burnt from slippage
business agent—union's area representative
can—scraper used to move earth; destroyer, U.S. Navy
Cat crankshaft—in make of diesel engine
cat pads—wide crawler tractor shoes for great bearing
  surface
Cat six governor—speed control unit on make of six
  cylinder diesel engine
Cheops Pyramid—butte
chuckawalla—lizard
Colonnade—North Rim point
compressor—machine that compresses air to power rock
  drills
compressor horn—air powered, used to signal
crane front—revolving power equipment with lattice boom
    fastened to deck frame used for hoisting
cut—excavation
dipper stick—lever arm connected to bucket, acts as
  fulcrum on revolving power shovel
dozer—crawler tractor equipped with bulldozer blade
drill doctor—air drill mechanic
Erie Fifty-one bucket—digging bucket on make of power
  shovel

Euc backdump—oversized dump truck
field superintendent—charge of construction site
fill rock—excavated rock used as fill
First Class—petty officer
Four Corners—common boundary to Colo., Utah, N.
    Mex., Ariz., once sacred place to area Indians
Gitmo—Guantanamo Naval Base
graveyard—work shift between 12 and 7 a.m.
Hall—union's local headquarters
hard hat—protective helmet
head walker—shift foreman
hedgehog—cactus
hoghouse—quarryman's shack with showers and lockers
hoist drum—clutch and brake controlled drum on power
    shovel and crane that spools hoist cable
house—deck, frames, power unit contained in body of
    crane
Humphreys and Sunset—extinct volcanoes
idling—engine running at idle speed
injectors—mechanisms that force fuel into diesel engine
    cylinders
Jimmie two-cycle—make of diesel engine
labor steward—worker representing his union's men on
    a job
master mac—head mechanic
muck—excavated material
na'le—deer
nonspin line—wire rope formed resistent to heavy
    strains that cause unwinding
oiler—helper on power shovel, oils and greases
Phantom Ranch—dude ranch at the bottom of Grand
    Canyon

Point Sublime—North Rim point
ponderosa, yellow pine—western pine
redwall—thick strata, marine deposition
swing—revolve power shovel, also assemblage to revolve
   house and boom
tagman—uses hand signals to show bucket's position in
   quarry when operator's sight is obstructed
Teec-nos-pos—first town southwest of Four Corners
teeth—socketed replaceable wearing edges on shovels
Ten-ten—make of power shovel, here with crane front
   (boom) attachment
Tonto—plateau above Inner Gorge
Traxcavator—make of crawler tractor with lift arms and
   bucket for digging and loading material
trip—release bucket latch for dumping
westcoast mirror—long rearview mirror
Wheels—navigator, U.S. Navy
whipline—hoist line
whiteface—hereford cattle
Whitehat—enlisted man, U.S. Navy
wire rope—cable
Wupatki—prehistoric ruins
xenos—stranger
zirk—grease fitting

IN MEMORIAM

George Browning Bronson

May 12 *October 8*
1898 *1965*

TRANSCANYON

Ponderosa cones
and needles duff groundcover,
morninglight insight.
Longdistance Father's
Day phonecall, his voice almost
and Gramp's one day gone.
Where'd you come from and
go to for eighty-seven years,
Gramp, if we're not there?
"You know what I am.",
my father's incarnate voice,
wept — voidlit stare.
Sunbeams on redwood
wallboard, blown window curtain
shadows around them.

MORROW, JOHN DONNE

Wife no help for one whom death is taking,
broken veins blacken skin, cheekbones protrude,
painful diseases fester, his want gone —
risen again and again each fresh breath;
no alternative but dereliction?

Last wait, isolation room's frail patient
worn-out coughing, still in hearkening calm,
milked white fingers build his temple rafters,
thumbs as kingpost and tips ridgepole nailed fast;
roofer over sternum pulses humbly . . .

Back home since then, "Why don't they let me go?",
she sleepless too, their bridal his deathbed
where first good morrow to their waking souls —
for love, one little room an everywhere;
the spirit everywhere same splendid room.

BURIAL THANKSGIVING

Eternal glory formlessly many forms,
no one became nor sixty-seven years
while he seemed so, dead among wife and sons
yet wholly creation — hardwood casket, sprays
of rust chrysanthemums and hemlock, grave's
dry oakleaves, grass shoots all illusion, not own.
Father, the corpse wants nothing just as earth
wants nothing, being heaven though unknown,
hallowed . . .   holy dead son, holy dirt
flung illuminant, pit holy dearth.

by R. S. Bronson, his son

THE AUTHOR

ROBERT STEVENS BRONSON was born in western Massachusetts, June 5, 1928. He graduated from the University of Illinois in 1950, afterward studying at Columbia University and the University of Michigan. Since 1954, when released from the Army, he has worked on construction.

THE BOOK

The text of this book was set on linotype in a typeface called PRIMER, a type cut by Rudolph Ruzicka. Ruzicka, a quality wood-engraver and book-designer, cut the type in 1947 at the request of *Linotype*. The attempt to produce a truly-up-to-date legibility face for a variety of needs resulted in the first size in metal, 12 pt., in 1949.

The book was composed and printed by THE ANN ARBOR PRESS, INC., Ann Arbor, Michigan; bound by THE DECKER BOOK BINDERY, Grand Rapids, Michigan. Typography by George Abbott White. Slipcover photograph by Robert Golden.

Photograph of the author by H. Ramsey Fowler.